HAMISH MACADRAM
by
JOHN COULL

Cover Designed by William Coull
Illustrations by John Coull

PUBLISHED BY NANCY COULL
1992

Hamish
MACADRAM
By John Coull

THIS STORY
MUST BE READ WITH A
HIGHLAND ACCENT

FOREWORD

I wish I had known John Coull, the author of "Hamish Macadram." He taught Science at Forres Academy for twenty years before dying of cancer a couple of years ago and he must have been rather a special human being because his family have gone to great trouble to have the book published. Only someone too of rather special imagination could have fathered such a friendly little brain-child of a book, wreathed as it is in warmth and humour.

Hamish Macadram's appearance in print is however, more than a memorial for a much-loved father and husband. It also constitutes an appeal to give generously to the Cancer Research Campaign (Scotland) because all profits will be directed towards this most deserving of charities to help provide a safe cancer-free Scotland. Recent progress is hopeful - enough to show that one day we'll know all the causes of cancer, how to prevent it, how to cure it. How near is that day? How many children and adults will suffer before cancer is conquered? Only intensive research can give the answer, research which needs money, your money to buy much needed equipment and the skill to use it.

If you're browsing over these words - in a whisky visitor centre, perhaps, or a bookshop - browse no longer. Take it to the sales assistant and buy it. You'll be supporting one of the most worthwhile causes in Scotland and giving yourself a treat at the same time. "Hamish Macadram" is like one of the fine malts which have inspired John Coull to write it- full of subtle character, gentle, amusing, distinctive. If you enjoy a wee sensation you'll enjoy "Hamish Macadram."

Stephen Robertson
of Scotland The What?

December 1991

Once upon a time there lived a Highlander called Hamish Macadram.

Heather growing

He lived with his wife and two kids Burt and Ben in a thatched cottage.

The smell in the house was terrible - it was all the kids fault but they did not seem to care.

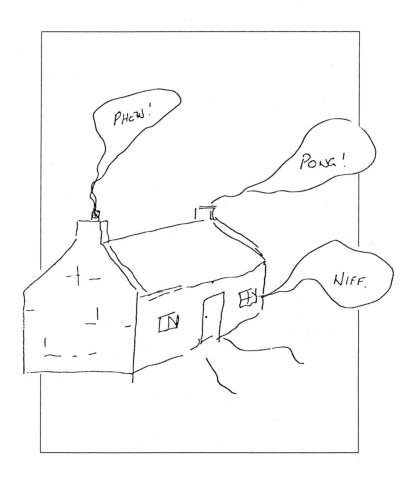

It got so bad his neighbours refused to visit his Burt
and Ben.

One dark night in sheer desperation, Hamish did away with Burt and Ben.

He was soon to regret it...

For three weeks there was nothing to eat but **GOAT - ROAST GOAT, CURRIED GOAT, GOAT BURGERS.**

He was fair scunnered. Oh! how he longed for a piece of roasted venison (even poached would do!)

H
amish was on the dole but his wife worked as the local mid-wife.

BABY DELIVERY SERVICE.

Since the three couples who lived in the glen were pensioners she had plenty of time on her hands - too much for Hamish's liking.

HAMISH !

Come here! I want you to cut peats, gather sticks, and help me in the kitchen

DRAT!!

(in gaelic)

T he thatched roof leaked.

They knew of one Thatcher but she lived too far away - far too far for her to bike and anyway, someone was always using it.

Buckets were scattered over the floor.

Hamish grew OATS and BARLEY with the
occasional THISTLE.

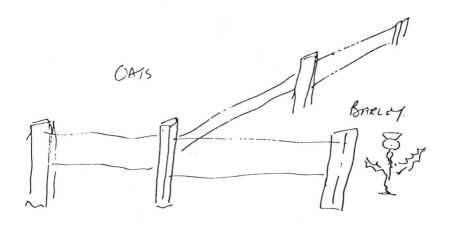

He liked his porridge made from Oatmeal.

This made him glow in the dark so he could read
his newspaper.

Hamish was not so fond of beer meal porridge so there was not much use for the Barley and he was beginning to wonder why he grew the stuff in the first place and even in the second place. Hamish stored some in a bucket and you can guess what happened - WATER got in to it.

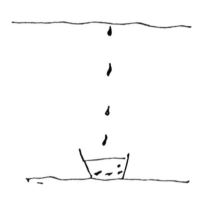

This made the barley sprout.

One day Hamish happened to be passing the bucket and feeling a bit peckish, he ate some of the barley. "Well, upon my sporran !" said Hamish. "They're sweet but a wee bit soggy."

He dried the barley over the peat fire and ate some
and put the rest into the bucket for later. Sure
enough, MORE water got into the bucket -
QUITE ALOT !

His wife made bread which she sold to the local
tearoom and Hamish had to help.

He was a bit slapdash, and lo and behold, a bit of
yeast plopped into the bucket.

A few days later Hamish happened to be passing the bucket and the brew was frothing away like

 mad.

It tasted yeasty, and had alcohol in it but what was he going to do with the froth?

Hamish had an idea! He said to his wife, "I think I'll give it a **WHISK,   EH** ?"

Now, his wife, poor dear, was slightly deaf. She thought that Hamish had said **WHISKY** !

The liquid was a bit cloudy,but he remembered how
to separate the alcohol from the liquor.
His Science Teacher would have been proud of him
as he fitted up the **STILL and WORM**

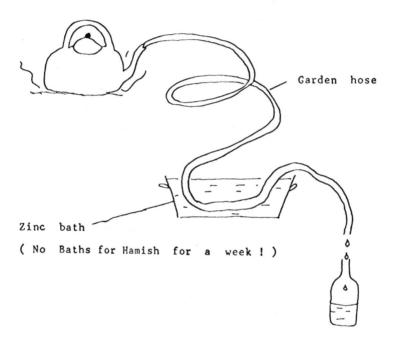

Garden   hose

Zinc   bath
(No   Baths for Hamish   for   a   week !)

Success was not the only thing that was going to
Hamish's head.
His whisky would do for celebrating the New Year
but as he had too much of it he sold some to the
neighbours.

Into the piggy bank went the money.
"Piggy Bank?   Boar Cash? **No - HOG MONEY!**"
mused Hamish.

What did his poor wife think he said?
You've guessed already— **HOGMANAY!**

He found that it cured colds and flu. It didn't really,
but it was a good excuse.

Hamish played the pipes and was a member of the local pipe band.

Returning one evening after practice, he dropped his chanter into a jar of whisky.

His wife, ever curious asked why.

"Well," said Hamish, "There's an epidemic of woodworm in the Hall and I don't want more holes in my chanter. I have enough bother with the ones already there!"

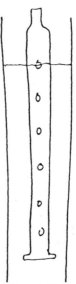

Now Hamish was a bright lad. He noticed that every time that the chanter always sank to the same level.

When asked how his whisky was doing, he would reply "Top hole! chust top hole!"

Amazingly, his playing of the chanter improved so much that he began winning prizes at the Mods.

One judge was overheard to say that he had never before heard the instrument played with so much spirit.

Hamish's "**HEEDRUM HODRUMS**" would echo round the hills.

After each performance he would carefully lower what he called his "**HEEDRUMETER**" into the whisky jar.

One of his problems was keeping his still out of sight of prying gaugers.

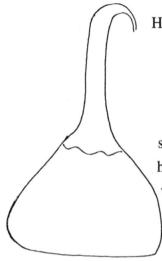

He painted it brown and green and passed it off as a giant onion, which he entered in the local Horticultural show.
The visiting Gauger was very suspicious. But, did Hamish not have green fingers? An attribute which seemed to be rubbing off on everything he touched.

The Fates were with Hamish when the Gauger tapped it with his stick.
"Well Hamish," he said, "You'll never win a prize with this onion."
"Why?" asked Hamish, the palms of his hands sweating, resulting in his fingers returning to their normal colour.

"Because it's boss in the middle!"

This was too much for Hamish who then applied for a distilling licence.

As the years passed his whisky improved and his business flourished, so much so that he decided to take a break and arranged a holiday through Skye Tours

Arriving late on Saturday there was not much to do but visit the bar where he could enjoy a dram of his own making. As usual the main topic of conversation was the weather and Hamish imagined what the forecast would have been in Noah's day...

"There will be continuous rain for a further 38 days and all travellers should heed the following warning.

ALL major roads are subject to severe flooding and are NOT advised, except for the following... The A939 Cockbridge- Tomintoul and the B..."

On the first morning, after breakfast, he settled into a deckchair to read a newspaper which he was unable to get back home - "The Spews of the World"

'Advanced Factory leased to Laxative Manufacturer. Local M.P. says it will create alot of jobs.'

It'll lead to the Highland Clearances, thought Hamish.

'A plague of boils hits Skye. It first affected the McDonalds and then the Camerons. The local doctor described it as a series of Clan Gatherings and said that the matter would soon be brought to a head. '
'**GYAD**' thought Hamish.

And what was this?
'Two ladies rowed the Atlantic, but one of them wasn't a lady. She was transvestite. They had left the mainland to cross to Skye but missed it.'
The heading in the local "Eaters' Digest" was "Two Too Teuch Teuchters" and there was a quote from one of the reception committee.

" I don't think much of the new-fangled Flora and as for Charlie, he was a bit too boney for me. I've swallowed umpteen tablets and have been wishing he would never come back again! So if you don't mind this is my last interview as I don't wish to bring the subject up again!"

Hamish read on...

"The Nobel Prize for Medicine was awarded to Mr.B. Sidebottom for developing an instrument for measuring the pressure in a patient's piles.

He called it a Haemorrhoid Barometer.

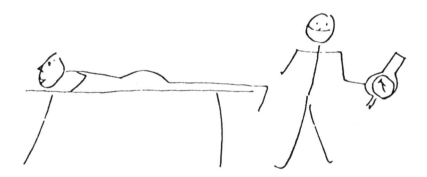

Hamish turned to the problem page, his favourite
wee read.

Dear Marge Frarts,
My love-life has been unexciting of late so I sent off
to a company for something "**GUARANTEED TO
PROVIDE EARTH MOVING
EXPERIENCES!**"

All I got was a **SHOVEL**!
Cau I sue this Company under the Trades
Description Act?
Yours Willie

No great shakes I'm afraid, Willie...
Marge.

As he was about to turn to the Sports pages he heard
a sound coming from the sea.
Scanning the waves he picked out a black bobbing
object.

At first Hamish thought that it was a seal but there being no Greenpeace ship around it couldn't be. Hamish wondered if there were to be dissention in the ranks would they be known as the 'split greenpeace movement'?

As the object drew nearer he identified it as a man clinging to a barrel.

Hamish had waded in until his kilt was floating horizontally in the water.

"I hope that no fish starts nibbling at my bait" mused Hamish, "Or a jellyfish with it's tentacles...that would be painful!"

Hamish dragged both the man and the barrel ashore. Apart from "Que" and "Si" and "Manuel" and "Real Madrid" Hamish could make little of what he was saying.
He must have fallen of a galleon, thought Hamish.

Hamish carried him to an Hotel - (a converted
Castle.) which had a reputation for making
everyone welcome and was known locally as

"Failte Towers."

It was also renowned for its seafood dishes - two in
particular -
Crab cooked in beer and called "Partan Special."
and the other, Fish cooked in a wine sauce
"Cod piece in tutu."

Hamish did not forget the barrel. After he had seen
to Manuel's comforts he went back to the shore to
collect it and when Hamish's holiday finished, both
Manuel and the barrel went home with him.

Manuel worked with Hamish for the rest of his days
and became as Hamish described him, his first
'**MANUEL**' labourer.

The barrel? It was now used to store whisky.

Hamish noticed that the whisky which was stored in the barrel had developed an attractive colour and it's flavour was much improved.

From that day on Hamish always kept a "Galleon of the best" for special occasions.

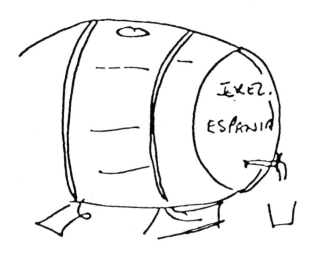

It was sometime later however before Hamish discovered how Manuel came to be floating in the sea clinging to a barrel...........

He had been with a party of tourists pony-trekking in Glen Shiel when they were set upon by a band of English soldiers. Manuel vividly described how a mixture of abject fear, beans for breakfast and an acceleration of 10g caused both he and his Irish horse Scarlet O'Mara, to leave a trail of farts as they made good their escape.

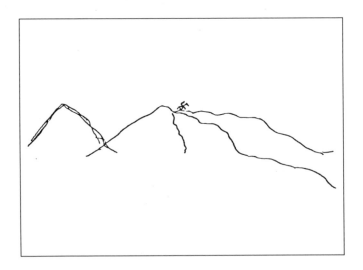

The English soldiers could only report to their Garrison that they'd 'Gone with the wind!'

For the rest of the day Manuel stayed on the saddle.

After dark, weary and sore, he stumbled on a small cottage by the shores of Loch Duich.

Apprehensively, he knocked on the door which was opened by a friendly woman who invited him in.

As he ate his supper from the mantle shelf his hostess rubbed his cheeks with "Oil of Islay."

"What a fine Pyr-o-nees you have! Mind you, you are Spanish. Ever thought of wearing the kilt?"

It had transpired that Manuel's hostess was none other than Mam Rattagan who lived with her five daughters but there was no Dad Rattagan. She was a warm hearted woman and many a weary traveller enjoyed her hospitality only to leave more weary in the morning. She and her daughters were a closely knit family and the Five Sisters remained in Kintail all their days. Their beauty was renowned and many a breathless admirer saught their affection.

Only two of their names were ever known, when the
following conversation was overheard.

In the fullness of time a son was born to Mam
Rattagan and much to the Locals' curiosity was
called "The Spaniard."

After staying the night Manuel left unwillingly in the morning, as he had to catch the boat at Kyle. While he relaxed on deck, the memories of the previous day occupied his mind.

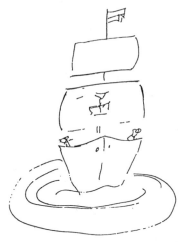

Suddenly, everything started spinning. At first Manuel thought it was the after-effects of his night with Mam Rattagan, but soon realised that the ship was caught in a giant whirlpool— the dreaded Corryvreckan. The ship, like all good ladies was older than was stated in the log book. As the captain said, "There are more miles to this galleon than you think!"

The ship was being sucked into this enormous black cauldron and with much creaking and groaning her ribs gave way. Manuel grabbed at the nearest object— a barrel of sherry. The liberal applications of the previous night of "Oil of Islay" prevented him from looking like a prune suffering from hypothermia.

And that was how Manuel came to be floating like an aquatic St. Bernard.

Over the years Hamish and Manuel spent many an evening swopping yarns whilst enjoying a dram of the amber distillate.

He informed Manuel that Highland dancing started when a practical joker put thistles under rush matting in the local Hall. This produced fiendish yells and much sporran bouncing! Despite the sole - searching and the pain, it's popularity spread and many Balls were held. **"OOCH!"** became **"HOOCH!"** and sporrans were adjusted.

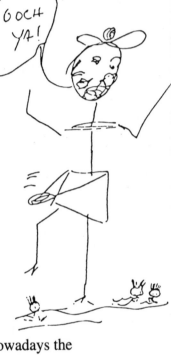

Nowadays the dancing was of two types...

One form was performed by those who were on the point of becoming legless and the other a more refined form...country dancing by what you might call **HOOCHTER TEUCHTERS.**

Manuel informed Hamish that it was a fellow with a verruca that introduced the Felluch, and that the local drooth after a horrendous binge and suffering the **DDT's** started stamping on imaginary cockroaches.

his antics were accompanied with shouts of
"FLAMING COCKROACHES"
(having previously removed his teeth.)

This was later shortened to "Flamin Co..." as he slowly slipped into unconsciousness.

Hamish had seen great changes in the Highlands, much of the land was now owned by gentlemen of Middle Eastern extraction.

Here, only pleasantries were exchanged across the river.

In winter when the loch was frozen over the locals
would hurl boulders aimlessly over the ice, until
Hamish presented a bottle as a prize. The person
who threw the boulder nearest the bottle won it.

The popularity of the game grew.

On the odd occasion that the bottle was accidently
broken, a brush was kept to sweep up the broken
glass and was known as the 'sliver broom.'
When the bottle was broken comments such as
"scotch on the rocks" and "I know I asked for ice
but this is ridiculous!" were heard.
One of the players - Johnnie Walker by name - not
one of the teachers, slipped and fell as he was
sweeping.

Unfortunately, another stone was on its way and
poor Johnnie became the first curler (but not the
last) to be stoned out of his mind!
When the deliverer enquired how he was, the skip
replied "Ach, he's nothing to Grouse about. He's
Cutties Sark but his Long John's OK!"

When poor Johnnie came round, he said, "You know Crawford, I keep seeing stars - sometimes three and sometimes five!

And who threw The **THUDDING STANE**?"

Hence Duddingston Loch became the home of curling.

As news of the wonder drink spread many visitors came to partake of "The Waters" and to live up a little.

Indeed so many visitors were arriving the Council approved the widening of the road and no expense was spared. At the opening ceremony every roadman had a new shovel to lean on.

GLEN"LIVEITUP"
WHISKY TRAIL

Hamish performed the opening ceremony and afterwards dispensed his usual hospitality so that everyone has "one for the road."

The glen became so famous that even the Eurovision Song Contest was held in the village hall - the one which the local "Clan Herald" claimed the winner was third cousin of Mrs. Grieg, No.2 the Glen. The competition was actually won by Norway, much to everyone's surprise. The winning song "Snegl Snegl kom ud af dit house." - "Snail Snail come out of your house." went down well with the continental juries, in particular the French, who awarded it full marks. Scotland's entry was sung by the Alexander Sisters - Bran and Anna - two great movers. The lyric was about a relative's bird being trapped in her loo. It was called "I've got a budgie in my cludgie!"

When the competition finished, all the competitors, composers and guests attended a Ceilidh - and some Ceilidh it turned out to be.

Brahms had a few drams, Beethoven had a fifth, followed by a sixth and finished one over the eight, Handel was turned on for he kept on shouting "Hallelujah", Mussorgsky made an exhibition of himself (which certainly wasn't Gudunov!), Debussy ended up on the roof serenading the moon, Ravel was confused, Verdi turned green, Hadyn was seek and Liszt was sober!

Hamish was not without his competitors.

There were the MacRumands but their product was not very popular. Eventually they were taken over by an American based multinational who gave it a new image and a new name ...."Macrumand Coke."

Even one of the middle-eastern gentlemen introduced a new brand the "Macallah" but somehow it just wasn't right!

I'd like to teach the world to drink

Hamish was by now famous. People worldwide drank his and their own health. He was honoured and in the New Year's Honours List was made a Lord and took the title 'Lord Macadram of Glenliveitup'

SAME KILT

NEW HEATHER

GLENLIVEITUP

Lord Macadram eventually made his way to London to take his seat and make his maiden speech. It was rumoured, quite wrongly, that Hamish went round singing "Soho my nut brown maiden."

One day during a lull in the proceedings Hamish imagined he heard the sound of sheep. Immediately his thoughts drifted back to the glen...... he was gathering...... he was clipping...... he was lambing (-not Hamish, the sheep was).

The urge to see the sheep was too great. he left the chamber, ran along the corridor and flung open the door.

Such was the blast of hot air which met him that
he was temporarily blinded by his kilt.

They weren't sheep, just MPs', pulling the wool
over the eyes of the electorate and invoking
taxes to fleece everybody.

This was too much for Hamish...

Back to the Braes of Glenliveitup he went, to spend
the rest of his days making whisky and playing his
pipes.

THE END

ISBN 0 - 9519174 - 0 - 4 HAMISH MACADRAM

Designed and Produced by McKENZIE ADVERTISING & DESIGN
Tel: (031) 229 7897